Aim High
or Die

"A True Detroit Story"

Images of a Lost
Dream..............

By, Angel Marino

Aim High or Die
"A True Detroit Story"

Published By, Angel Marino &

Aim High Productions LLC,

Detroit, MI. 48238

Aimhigh313@gmail.com

This Book or parts thereof may not be reproduced in any form, stored in retrieval system or transmitted by any means-electronic, mechanical, photocopy, recording or otherwise-without prior written consent or permission of the publisher, except as provided by the United States of America Copyright Law.

Cover Design By, Decarlos Stewart

Interior Design By, Angel Marino

Copyright© 2011

Aim High Productions LLC

All rights Reserved

ISBN# 978-0-615-46007-9

Printed in the United States of America

Aim High or Die
"A true Detroit story"

To Demi EllA ROSE

Michael Fitzgerald MD

Jahi, Thank you for wisdom

BLESSED

RIP
Demeatrice Exie Marino "Dee Dee"

My Father Norman Benge

Granny Eleanor Marino Laidler

Professor Charles Redmond

E HOB Photo man

Erichobson.smugmug.com
Hobson media group "HMG"
Uncle D
All my Friends & Loved ones

ALKEY ENTERTAINMENT GROUP

Thank you God for Jesus

Images of A Lost Dream

Aim High or Die
"A true Detroit story"

Contents

Preface.. .
Introduction:
Road to Aim High..

<u>Attempt 1</u>

Childhood Nightmares.......................................

<u>Attempt 2</u>

My Mother is Dead...

<u>Attempt 3</u>

September 11, 2001..

<u>Attempt 4</u>

New Orleans...

<u>Attempt 5</u>

New York, New, York
..

<u>Attempt 6</u>
I'm a Mother
now..
<u>Attempt 7</u>
I'm A Star- Aim High A Victor........................

Images of A Lost Dream

Aim High or Die
"A truf Detroit story"
Preface

In America the land of the Free,

the home of the Brave, the Blueprint of Democracy for other countries, we the people are entitled to many rights; perhaps the most important of these is Freedom of Speech, and the right to have our own opinions. America is populated with many different racial backgrounds, several religions, heterosexuals, homosexuals, and transsexuals; therefore we are prone to many different and all too many extreme beliefs, behaviors, opinions, and unfortunately, stereotypes. I ask myself, "How does it really work, who's wrong and who's right; is there a wrong and a right?" I wonder are we Americans at all any different from Dictatorship countries, are we actually the country to model, and to be absolutely honest what makes us any different from third world extreme countries that we find ourselves occupying, freeing, and trying to relieve. The answer is excessively complex to sum up in a yes or no answer; this is going to take real life views such as my very own that I will soon relay and those of others from every corner of this "Great" country. Let us start by my introduction to you the reader. Hello, my name is Angel Marino and I am a twenty-eight year old, African-American, Black, minority, woman, of obvious Cuban descent, who lives in an urban area, Ghetto, Hood, or whatever you would like to label it, neighborhood. However important those few demographics are, this is not an autobiography, but rather a thesis on moral perceptions, and how all too many times, our differences result in

Aim High or Die
"A true Detroit story"

violence, hate crimes, social separation, prejudices, discrimination and ultimately how we the American people, fail at being the blueprint of Freedom, Democracy and the land of the free. If you believe in Jesus as I do then you understand the reasoning behind my beliefs that this book will not only change my life but those whom I love and others who need to know that they are not alone. Life is what you make it. Whether the glass is half-empty or half-full depends upon how you perceive it to be. I pray that I can help people to see that it is up to us to seek out our own truths, and Dream as big as possible, because the possibilities are endless. If a Door is closed open it, if it is open go through it and if you do not see the Door keep looking and you will find that it was in you from the beginning.

"Aim High Time Flies", "Get your life right"

is one of my original quotes; I not only wish to relay that message but to live by it and to become an example of it to the World.

This Book has been a long time in the making; I always knew I wanted to tell my Mother's life story. There are so many victims in this story, but the message is ultimately to become a victor and not remain a victim.

"This book is my Truth and my Light and my way to Freedom from the captivity that has held my spiritual being in Bondage. I pray that it also allows my Mother's soul to indeed Rest in Peace, the term we use so lightly."

Images of A Lost Dream

Aim High or Die
"A true Detroit story"

INTRODUCTION

This book is dedicated to my late Mother, Demeatrice Exie Marino, who reminds me of a bird, a free flying bird.

Aim high or Die is the most important project that I have created and attempted to finish. I hold it dear to my heart for many reasons. First, it is important that I finish something for once in my life. I have to find a way to stop living in the clouds, in my dreams, waiting for lady luck to come and save the day. Second, it is most important, because my mother isn't around to tell her own short yet full-filled story so that this may possibly assist to help avoid this horrific event which continues to happen so often now in this day and time. I want other motherless swans such as abused women, other women and myself who have yet to be abused, to know that I am here and I understand. You are not alone in this fight. There are many others who can relate to your situation. This book also is dedicated to other motherless children; keep your Aim High in order to reach your highest potential. This book is meant for women from everywhere in the world, far and near, of every race and religion. My mother's life was tragically taken like those of so many other women in the world. Domestic violence needs to stop. This book I hope will

Aim High or Die
"A true Detroit story"

save someone's life; someone who feels trapped, who feels abandoned, or who has no self-esteem. I say fly, fly like a soaring eagle, and never let anything get in your way. Life is too short and we have but one time around to make it right. Your children will never rest, and I will never rest until my job is done, to heal, and also to love, to motivate, and to inform our peers of the pitfalls of love and the downside of love triangles. In doing so we will provide support, and hopefully change for the millions of women who have no idea what loving you is and the signs of an abusive partnership.

"Mother, if you can hear me, I am sorry that your life was taken. Although I cannot bring you back in the physical, I will never let you die in spirit. I know that you could sing like a bird and aspired to do great things. I know this because I feel it running through my veins. I will see it through; even if I should die in the balance, because the life that I know is only because of you. Your motivation, your blood, it takes me over and I become so emotional but also I think, rational. This is from the heart; it is true and it is genuine." I figured someone out there in the world could relate to your life and learn from your death.

Aim High or Die
"A true Detroit story"

"Please Mother do not worry, try to rest in peace; because I will meet you on the other side. I will see you again. I will hear your voice. I believe that, that is what keeps me motivated, what pushes me out of bed every day. That is why I am writing right now. I hope that I have not let you down, and I pray to God that I can make Him proud of me; so proud that I can be with you and Him. Therefore, even though It seems like you died, you are alive in me. Every time someone turns the page in this book and you take a breath and inhale, I will exhale. You are alive and well. I love you."

This book is also dedicated to the Ainesmon family. The reason why I dedicate this book to you as well, is because I believe in forgiveness and because of the pain and suffering that you had to face when your Son, Nephew, Brother, or Cousin, murdered my mother. For many years, Mrs. Ainesmon, I believe, went around the community with her head down; ashamed and alone in the neighborhood and in the community because your son made you all seem like bad people. We met a few times in my adulthood, Mrs. Ainesmon, at a church event; you seemed so eager to tell me how sorry you were and asked me for a hug. I gave you a hug without even questioning why. I forgive your son and

Aim High or Die
"A true Detroit story"

I hope that you can too. It is okay. I will find you and send you a copy of this; once again I am okay I am blessed and I am ready now. Last but not least, this book is dedicated to my Father, Granny, and precious Daughter, Demi Ella Rose Marino who have always believed in me and has encouraged me to pursue my Dreams and who will be there for me no matter what happens in life, so thank you both for providing me with something more important than the air I breath, love and family. Love always your Mother, Daughter and Granddaughter. Love you Demi.

AIM HIGH OR DIE
"A TRUE DETROIT STORY"
IMAGES OF A LOST DREAM
ATTEMPT 1
CHILDHOOD NIGHTMARES

This is the first attempt to finish what I started many years ago; I thought that I had it so bad. You know, you never quite understand why things are so bad, you never ask for it, but what happens is, one day you realize it and you have no choice but to suck it up because this is the way it is. I was a twenty-one year old college student in debt to my neck. I had at that point, "debt to my neck and all", achieve everything and more of what was expected of me. As far back as I can remember, (as a

Aim High or Die
"A true Detroit story"

matter of fact) one of my first memories, almost as if my life began when I was seven, was having a birthday party, and I can remember everyone looking at me with big grins and smiles on their faces singing happy birthday. I had a mother, a father, a younger sister and baby brother.

I knew I was treated a little bit differently than my siblings. I tended to believe I was being handled with care. I would soon find out that I was being pitied upon. In the beginning, it seemed like everything was going to be good.

Oh, by the way, my name is Angel Irene Marino. I was born and raised in Detroit Michigan, the motor city, and the home of Motown Records. My mother, Demeatrice Marino, and father Norman Benge became parents, yet they were still teenagers living with their parents whose marriage had been arranged due to a circumstance, that of course being me. My father, Norman Benge, was a bus boy at Trapper's Alley oyster bar; pretty boy charisma, pumped waves, light skin, and this was in the 80's. My father was a walking ghetto celebrity, with his cool charm, and humanitarian ways. Therefore, it does not take a rocket scientist to figure out why he had to attain my mother as a sort of asset. In his own words, he said that when he first laid eyes on my mother that he felt he had to make the prettiest girl in the school his woman. My Mother Demeatrice was an inspiring singer who had made her stamp on the community so to speak; singing with the church choir, and with other groups. One of them was the "Floaters" of Detroit Michigan. She was studying to get her nursing certification and also working as a Teacher's assistant at

Aim High or Die
"A true Detroit story"

Zion Lutheran. I think I can remember her at the day care. I was one of the babies she was being paid to watch over, maybe with a little borrowed time perhaps. My parents, I believe, were victims of the time era, the fads, the drugs, and basically, all the elements that caused the epidemic of HIV/AIDS, crack cocaine, the gangs of the 1980's such as Young Boys Inc., Pony Down, the Errol Flynn's, and many others. My Mother, a beautiful woman, with light–skin, long wavy black hair, and a voice like a bird was hated for being confident, which sometimes came off as "arrogance" and self-esteem which sometimes came off as "thinking your better". Like most arranged marriages, where the bride and groom are teenagers, the possibility of exploring can be a little alluring. That is what happened. My father had many other women and my mother discovered other men. It turned out that a child-hood friend and grandson to my great-granny's neighbor would fall so madly in love with my mother, that he would shoot my twenty-year-old mother that day of June 27, 1985 with a twelve gauge sawed off shotgun several times. Did I mention in the same home as her Nate (grandmother) and poppa (grandfather) and questionably myself. The reason for the question is that I have been told different accounts of the story from both sides of my family. My mother's side may be trying to protect me and my father's side might be trying to tell me the truth. Well it really does not matter what either side has told me because I have my own God given clips, as I like to call them, of images embedded in my head. The truth is I did not understand that my mother was dead and the family I thought I had, was an attempt to give me one. My father and stepmother would soon divorce, and more important, now I was motherless for the first time at the age of ten. Even though my mother had been deceased since I was

Aim High or Die
"A true Detroit story"

two. My granny, my mother's, mother was influential in my life and always will be. My granny waged a strong tooth and nail battle to win the custody case that they now faced. My father's family would egg my father on about fighting for custody for his daughter Angel, his baby girl, despite the fact that he probably was not in the best condition to take on the responsibility of raising me all by himself. I guess I cannot even begin to imagine what he had to be going through at that horrible time in his life, and in the lives of everyone involved. My father probably thought that if he would just let my granny raise me, that he would never see me again. My granny, I believe was under the impression that my father was nothing but a young gang member with no job and could not possibly take care of her grandbaby. Well, my granny would be shocked to find out that my father had gone and married a lady name Tonya, who would testify in court, under oath, that she would indeed be with my father; that they had eloped and that she had a full-time job working for the state. Custody was awarded to my father; that was the end of the end, for from that moment forward, I was never in a stable home. I was as a charity case, passed along from aunt to aunt. I even stayed with a few uncles, friends, and eventually a boyfriend. I am here to tell you there was no worse feeling than watching my Father to leave with me in the care of his family. I believe he felt that I would be better off with them. What he did not understand is that I would rather have suffered with him; like the nights he carried me on his back in a blizzard to the market to get something to eat for a few bucks. The nights we slept in that family flat on Monterey and Dexter with no locks on the doors. My Father would cook a three-course meal all at once in an electric pan. The times he dressed me in his clothes and

Aim High or Die
"A true Detroit story"

insisted that, I looked great. The times he brushed my hair in a ponytail and the mornings he gave me forty cents for my reduced free lunch. Those were the moments I knew my father loved me. I do not know if my father will ever recover from the killing of his first wife, in his own words, maybe he provoked it a little bit, His second love dying of leukemia and him not being a match for her to live, and his third wife leaving him and his young daughter, me, for another woman. Yes, I said it a woman. That is how and when it all began, the drop offs. My Father one night, I will never forget this day, it was a cold winter night and Tonya had just left us; my Father practically begged me to go with her and my stepsister. I was afraid. I was scared, and most of all I wanted to be with my dad. Well, he told me that he could not handle the responsibility of raising me. I do not think at that young age I quite understood what he meant, but of course, now I know that he meant he could not raise a little girl by himself. He then proceeded to tell me that he would be taking me to his sister's house.

I was happy, I wanted to see my cousins; but when we arrived, I remember feeling like this was not going to be for a couple of days or the weekend. My aunt said to my dad, "no, no Norman" a million times to my Father, they were whispering. I remember her telling him "I cannot Norman." He said to forget what she said and forget that I am begging him to let me stay with him. He leaves. She said "come on in Angel", took me upstairs to her daughter's room, and put me in the bed with her daughter. As soon as the lights were turned off, she said "if you pass this pole, I am kicking your ass." You see, when living with my aunt's family, I was introduced to the reality that many children are privileged to have had fancy clothes, shopping sprees, gifts, birthday parties, and christmas presents. These things meant

Aim High or Die
"A true Detroit story"

nothing to me until I was living with other kids, my cousins, who were showered with these things; their parents, my aunts, were addicted to shopping every weekend and of course they wanted their kids to have nice things. Believe me, these things are much easier to understand as an adult, rather than when I was expected to understand as a child. I mean for crying out loud; I was bringing home good grades, and running track, and participating in most of the school functions; but when it was time for a ceremony, no one was there. When it was time for a track meet, city finals, no one was there to document my accomplishments or simply to be of some support. I think these are some of the reasons why I am sort of bitter, but at the same time so loving and understanding. I am not mad at the man who killed my mother, nor at my aunt who tortured me and cut my long hair. I would have rather have said "ruined myself esteem," but I know that is not the case here. I can barely watch television sitcoms; I am always connecting myself to other people's families, heartbreaks, lost or even happy moments, like holidays, marriages, and giving birth. I tend to believe that I am the only one who cries and who has nightmares.

About Me: By Me

You've have no idea how many people ask, no, I am not related to Dan Marino; which would probably be nice but I am single and legal age and I hope to one day get married. I have yet to have children; I expect I will someday. I work as a server, because it is an opportunity to meet people in the world in many different aspects. Everyone has to dine out at some point. I have been in school 3 years majoring in communication. I hope to one day become involved

Aim High or Die
"A true Detroit story"

with the media somehow as an anchor, or a sports journalist for the news or something like that. I have many hobbies, reading, and writing poetry, and of course hanging out. My favorite food is seafood, lobster and shrimp. I believe my future has lots to offer, and that there are awards to come. I will continue to be the best person I can be.
This is something I wrote sometime in my first attempt of college days.
Nevertheless, boy how easily distracted I can become from all the skills and talents that I have, and totally lose track of my goals by becoming an emotional wreck and being unable to function. Hey, what better example than this comedic attempt to make what was going on at that time funny? My instructor at Wayne state asked us to write a paper about anything using all the words given us on a piece of paper.

If I recall correctly, it was about one hundred.
Here it goes!
{"The road was tuff and the time went slowly as if it could not be no worse for the student. It was apparent that the young women had and argument recently because she was telling everybody everything and all the juicy details. Between you and me, instead of broadcasting information however I please we will carefully compare and contrast the issues. Undoubtedly, due to finance issues she agrees to pay an outstanding bill and suggests that she pays it in full. She also acknowledges that she will never be late again and if she was that, they evict her from her apartment. The leasing manager offers her to sit the

Aim High or Die
"A true Detroit story"

semester out until she can pay her bill. Anything but a semester off the student cried out, on the other hand, wait a manger said. She states that she would not mind but there hard to find. To summarize the scenario I need your immediate attention the leasing manager argues. Until I can see, you are working and bringing in some money, we will not lift your hold. Many things I cannot accept the cause and effect cannot compare to their reactions. I believe that she was very dependent and granted that she knows nothing more. In fact, in other words she is a crybaby, asserts, and charges at people when things do not go her way. She criticizes the housing unit, declares that they work with her, and reports to the president of the university. In addition to that, she makes the human race look bad because she does not pay her bills. Due to the awfulness her professor advises her to keep writing for her chances are among the best. I also dropped in on a conversation that was too good to be true; truly, I heard that she was pregnant. All right, let us see pregnancy in college is certainly not good. She in fact takes a visit to the nurse so that she can find out if she really is pregnant. Instead of telling her parents, she does whatever is necessary to stay in school. With no parenting skills and no money and no apartment how would she do it? They classify her as a failure because she fell beneath against the storm. Something emphasizes to me that human kind are so much like children and that we now by way of destruction will kill ourselves off. That confirms nothing at all because that was a quote from "I robot" sunny the robot. I can bet there is somebody that feels the same excessively. Early January the student was particularly happy before all the occurrences had occurred she was in her apartment with no one but her cat. A loud knock at the door in addition to

Aim High or Die
"A true Detroit story"

"police officer" namely got her attention. Nevertheless, she has not committed a crime and opens the door. Otherwise, she would have seemed suspicious. For instance when they stop you on a routine stop if you run that is a sign of guilt.

Define loud music. First, the radio must be on. In the meantime, they advise her to turn the radio down. Over the past few days except during that time, other people below him definitely complained. The officer disagrees with the student. He describes a very different story and claims her to be disorderly. The other attendant confirms and interprets that she was not the problem he was. By way of telephone from the county lock up, she loses her sense of stability, or anybody else would call it a break down. Personnel from the lock up tried to help her whether a not she wanted help or not and in conclusion she allows them.

In front of the judge, the chair and the chairperson she finally gets a chance to explain herself. After they analyze evidence, they have yet to arraign her. Overall, hand they reports to the court a delay for a list of file was missing. That gave the defense attorney a chance to ask and for her to answer questions. Her answers were a way of success to separate fact from fiction. They have already developed their theories. The mail carrier the engineer from Wayne state and a flight attendant who held damaging testimony where ready for court. Does anybody object? In the environment where the student apartments there are so many people playing loud music the flight attendant said, under oath. Every day I try to exercise with peace and sleep but their all-playing music, the engineer said. I said this is final. What did you do said the prosecutor? I looked for immediate help. Maybe I am a little nosy but that building needs management. The mail carrier cried out. Finally, I asked to be relocated. Beside that, can you recall

Aim High or Die
"A true Detroit story"

loud music coming from apartment seven? Yes, I can say that. The judge objects to that response. Your remarks are getting out of hand counsel. The student therefore became successful another way keeping her business her business. Meanwhile there is nothing nowhere or nobody that can stop this young student from being whatever it is she wants to do. She might even want to take up writing like me. In addition to this, she is still trying to finish school keep people out her business and me the reporter on juicy gossip on campus."}

Wow! You see that is amazing. This and many other pieces that I have written are signs of a good time in my life. Whenever I can write or am writing for that matter, I feel great. I feel lifted and closer to the true me. God is the most important man in my life. I am only twenty-three years old, just 6 months away from twenty-two and I have already out lived my mother by two years. Wow! That is amazing. It wasn't easy coming up as a child, but it seems as though it gets worse as I become a woman. I think about my wedding day, and I think about the day I give birth to a child; and more importantly when I think about the childhood I never had, the unconditional mothers love that I never experienced from my own mother the way she would have loved me.

Thanks Aunt Donita

Let me share a poem that I wrote if you do not mind!

Aim High or Die
"A true Detroit story"

A mother's love

There is nothing on earth like mother's love
It is pure in heart and sent from above

It is rich in blessings

Calling on the lord to protect her family

Her blessings are answered

Because a Mother's love is true in faith
A mother's love makes no mistakes

A mother's love

Raises the best children

Who raises their children?

In addition, their children have children

It is a continuing cycle

You do not have to have a mother

Or may have lost your mother

Aim High or Die
"A true Detroit story"

but she always remains

Because her blood is running through your veins

So I thank your mother

Who gave you the love?

To be able to give a mother's love

There is nothing in this world

That I hold so dear

Like the motherly advise
You have whispered past my ear.

The special memories I hold so dear

The times when you have erased my fear

The undying love that lasts forever

and the precious moments we've spent together

I have seen many children abuse the unconditional love that only a Mother can give, and I have seen many despise the

Aim High or Die
"A true Detroit story"

conditional love that a Father gives you. Well my only input is that the Bible says to honor your Mother and Father. My mother is being honored at this very moment as I tell my story and in doing so, I am telling hers. Many loved my mother. Her death was a death to a whole family and members of the community.

When she got killed June of eighty-five, three of her family members my great grandfather poppa, who was there in the home when she got killed, my uncle junior, and my uncle bobby, were devastated along with the entire family. My Big Daddy I am sure has a void in his heart. Poppa's death was definitely pre-mature due to a broken heart. She meant so much to so many people in her life. However, I find that it means most to me to honor her life and to not let her die. She came up short but her impact and love are so long. This is for you Mother. Not having a Mother I tended to find that love or at least thought it was that kind of love, through men. I would find out the hard way after having been lied to, after having been dumped, after having been told I could not have my babies because he was not ready.

I was looking for a friend in a man.

Aim High or Die
"A true Detroit story"

<u>I was looking for a friend in a man.</u>

You wear your heart on your sleeves

Granny jeez!

However, that will be the death of you

In addition, you must remain true

In addition, in doing so I let go I gave it all

Whatever it took to answer the calls

Many ways and many days spent

Trying to convince

Trying to save all in his name

And look what I've gained
Backs turned against

No one in the physical tense

Aim High or Die
"A true Detroit story"

Here is my cry

No one to give me a ride or lend me a hand

Alternatively, possibly bake bread

I opened my doors

I gave my keys

And more importantly

My soul has suffered my spirit is weakened

I can use some special prayer from the deacons

Now I am thinking..................

My conscious is my friend

When my hand gets to tingle and my mind is out of control

Just like that driver

Therefore, I ask to be put out on the road

Well I have been put out better places

And been called far worse names

Images of A Lost Dream

Aim High or Die
"A true Detroit story"

My conscious is the one that tells me cool remain

"Love don't love nobody", "why do fools fall in love"

Well granny said, "Love is what love does"

And frankly, no one is doing anything for me

So you see

You got to, "have a self to give a self"

And that is what I lost

Know my right cheek pays the cost

My self-esteem is shattered

All that matters is my education

And keeping motivation to write

Because along with my conscious it is truly my friend

Time and time again we meet to exchange information

From the depths of my soul

The future untold but revealed

Images of A Lost Dream

Aim High or Die
"A true Detroit story"

When my hand entangles with the pen

And I was looking for a friend

In the meanwhile, "God has a child that can hold it's on"

And faith is worth nothing if I do not hold on

Side-tracked for a minute but evolved back to the core

And too astray from the true calling would be taboo

Strive to stay true to the real you

EMOTIONS…………………

Control your emotions

Is the poison

To living your dreams

It seems so unreachable

You are living it

The little things

Aim High or Die
"A true Detroit story"

Please wake up

Exhale

Thank the universe for whatever you have

Give back

Eat

Work

Play

Don't you ever be sad?

It's precious some say short

But I'm not counting

Its new day

Thank Yahweh

I am dancing laughing and shouting

You are what you have

Not true

Aim High or Die
"A true Detroit story"

You are what you do

What you produce

What you grow

Raising up

To be green and ripe

So you may reap from your own fruits

Not what you see

Bare all that you can assume

Change the content on the news

Use all the paper

And the ink out the pen

Every space blank

So your message is in

Here in full color

Aim High or Die
"A true Detroit story"

Red white and blue

Black green and red

Rose colored

Blind

Because it's all good

Mother earth to guide you out the hood

Were soldier in this war

With a powerful source

Tell it to them

In a beautiful voice

Remind them their choice

Get up right no

Wake up stand up

Stand up for your life

Never question why

Aim High or Die
"A true Detroit story"

And may all the blessings be unto you

As you control your life, thinking up a great way of living, a new beginning a new day...

When I was coming up I tried to keep myself busy with school functions. At that point I had no idea whether I wanted to be a future teacher, or a cross guard, or on the junior Olympics, I was an all-round student. I never knew that I was pursuing school activities because I had no home; school was my home. The teachers, the staff, and even some of the students, became closer to me than my own family. Speaking of students, I would like to take this time to thank Franchise, Dennis, Kwanza, Rickie, and Isaiah for being my friends and more importantly being a family to me. I don't know where I would be right now without them. Wow! God has made a way for me. There are many other people who I would like to thank for having had a vital hand in enabling me to do what I do today. Michelle, I haven't forgotten about you and the Robinsons. Thank you for my brothers, and thank you for displaying my track trophies as though I were your very own. Thanks for helping develop me into a woman. Uncle Darryl I know it was nothing to you and Tracey, but you didn't have to take in your niece, when you were a young newlywed, but thank you. I love you. Auntie Cindy and uncle D thank you too. Thanks for the ride to school. Thank you, Auntie Kima, Zima, Debra, and Gi Gi girl. You know that I love you all, and thank you too for providing me a home over the years even if some things I still have no understanding of; I now lean not on my own understanding. Thank you,

Aim High or Die
"A true Detroit story"

Tina Williams and the Williams family. Thank you for loving me, providing for me, not judging me, and for encouraging me to do something with my life by going to college and so much more. I do not know how I will begin to pay you all back but thank you so much. I believe that God used you all to help me. It is not at all easy writing this without tears running down my face. I pray to God that if I had a child and something was to happen to me that my child would be just as blessed, as I was to have so many people there to help. Well, while I'm thanking people; thank you Cooley high, thank you Mrs. Crowder, thank you SGT. Matthews, thank you Mr. Unabu, thank you Mrs. Edwards, thank you Mr. Dickens, thank you Mr. Halliburton, and thank you Mrs. Jones for helping me develop my English skills. If it were not for all these people pulling and pushing me, I really don't know where I would be. What would I have to write about? What passion would I have? How can I forget Mr. Iwankovitsch, my tenth grade government class teacher? Thank you for showing me how to channel my energy into poetry and for failing me for being disruptive because, in your words, I asked questions and wanted answers. Maybe you didn't have the answers, but you just couldn't say that. Thanks for playing race riot video clips during Black History Month and making me angry because the book taught us that Blacks and the poorest were second-class citizens. At that time I had no idea that you were a Jewish man or even what it meant to be Jewish, the Holocaust, and the fact that your race was put through pain and suffering for years as well. You played a video called revisiting the dream, and gave us an opportunity to write what we felt about it in the form of an essay. This is what I wrote.

Images of A Lost Dream

Aim High or Die
"A true Detroit story"
REVISITING THE DREAM

I am sick of going to school

To be played as a fool

Go to class and see a video

Of a black man kissing the white man's ass

Who in the hell wrote the rules?

The ones who make them

Are the ones who break them?

Why do we learn the history of getting our ass beat?

Is it because they want us mad to want revenge?

or is it because they just don't want this hate to end

We learn about the white man all year through

and in the shortest month of the year we suppose to celebrate black cheer

What is a first class citizen?

The rich man, or the white man?

Because my skin is not white

And my pocket not fat

You try to hold me back

Aim High or Die
"A true Detroit story"

But my skin is black

and my blood is rich

and where I'm going

I will pick

All this hatred and fear

The end of the world is near

We all are doves and treating each other like vultures

Nope this is not right this is torture

"And I turned to my class members and said"

We fought all this time to have a seat on the front of the bus

but every time we get on we run straight to the back

A lack of a black leader's strength and courage you see

doesn't all this hatred makes you want to scream?

I am mad as hell

And just revisiting the dream!!!!!!!!!!!!!!!!!

Aim High or Die
"A true Detroit story"

Well I got to go to summer school for free that year and eventually got the "a" that I had earned in the regular school year. He proceeded to tell me that I was a smart young lady but there was a time and a place to say the things that I said. Well, I felt there was no better time and place than early and in school. That's what a hearty breakfast will do for a young, eager, and curious, mind such as my own; definitely at that time in my life. I was looking for answers to everything. Why was my mother killed, why were we considered second class, and why was I not like the other kids. I wrote that when I was about fifteen years old. Most of my peers were interested in clothes and boys, not in writing poetry I think I was about fourteen years old when Caviar introduced me to my talent. I had been doodling little sayings on paper, questioning many theories, and basically pouring out my frustrations in the form of poetry for about a year at that point in the hallways at school, and in the silence of the hallway at the top of my auntie Kim's stairs. I was embarrassed to be writing in a way because everyone else was doing "normal" things. You know like jumping on the trampoline, riding bikes, and playing games; I think that maybe I was an ill, sad, child. I remember my aunt asking me what was wrong with me. I would say nothing and they would respond," well smile then." He kept on bribing me to go with him on Wednesday nights to Coca's House of Comedy for an open MIC session. I wasn't even old enough to get in the place. We got stopped at the door and Caviar told Coca that I was his niece and you've got to hear her. Despite the fact that it was a bar, she allowed me to do my poem. I had no idea what was going to happen I was very scared, but the

Aim High or Die
"A true Detroit story"

reaction I would get would soon prove me to be good at this spoken word thing!!!!!!!   It went like this.

The Will

Will succeed it's a need

Believing in trust and us

Conveying the image I want others to remember

January through December

Night and day my way

Money what could it bring

Maybe the cries of your mother the way a canary sings

I mean money is power all people can't handle

Power to do what you may have your way

Hate makes you evil and pity makes you gay

Money brought you aids because you had the price to lie

Take over the land make bread or end up dead it's said

End a crack fiend sick to your brain

Your money brought you drugs and now you're insane

Not so strong out on cane money make you hate

Aim High or Die
"A true Detroit story"

Depending on the way you relate you see

Everyone who is trying to take has made a mistake

You're mad and the whole worlds glad out for your head

Sleep tight at night money made you soft

Because you felt you should floss but it's managed

That's how to get cabbage

Grow enough to feed all your silly rabbits

The diamond in the rough is forced to be as tough

As any given Sunday you want to test my luck

Or to put me thru anything more than what I've got to do

Straight striving to earn

You'll never be handed what you deserve it's learned

Have you ever meet a young one just like me

Living and realizing the reality

A real friend sister daughter and granddaughter

Searching for the answer of my mom being man-slaughtered

When will it pay in the good book say one day?

So I' ill trust that and be on my way

I'm misunderstood to people I know

People everywhere I go people in the streets

Aim High or Die
"A true Detroit story"

Everyone has his or her own theory of me

I don't hate them just take them

Using them as sources

Another notation to help me through these courses

My life is in night school all through the day

Seeming to meditate about reality and if it's coming my way

To find the best way that I can say is brighten my ways

Amazing how I love and thug

Emotions hung up so I trust that I must stay alert on earth

Staying true to my name making it threw the rain

My life's dark but my future days bright

I'm smooth on good days and struggling through the nights

It's all right still learning a lesson through all my testing

Admitted and repented for my sins my story has just begun its preparing me to handle my own

When the lights turned out your peoples lost were

Your cousin's when you're balling

When you're fallen there not calling

Reality strikes you want haters out of your life

That's a piece of game to solve the mystery world of pain

Aim High or Die
"A true Detroit story"
It's how you'll teach who to trust it's in my will it's a must.

Boy was I deep at a young age frustrated and angry.

  I had nothing to be happy about then, everything was family oriented, and I knew that mine wasn't complete. Having never really had a stable home, I believed at the time, really wasn't affecting me, but I did not have a clue that it would influence my entire life; giving me the motivation to have something, and to never, if God willing I have a child, allow this to happen to mine. So many things happened, things that even now that I am obligated and supposed to dish out in this book seems too much to bear. Being verbally and physically molested, and abused by close people to me, who I loved and trusted. Neglect beyond measure from family that should have had my interests at heart. Simply feeling at many times like, why go on, why try to be good when no one cared. Thanksgiving, Christmas, Easter Sunday, these were the worst for me and are still hard to this day. There was one thing that not only made me smile and sometimes cry, but brought me close to my mother; the sound of music. Music is the window to the soul, and many songs are as if my mother is actually singing to me. The melody of beautiful music reminds me of a safe place. It makes me wonder if that is what heaven is like. Without music, I have no star gate to the other side so to speak. I am like a wingless bird, or a fish with no gills. I know that God has given me the

Aim High or Die
"A true Detroit story"

gift of music interpretation and song as memories that have gradually, and all so tragically taken root in my heart.

AIM HIGH OR DIE

"A TRUE DETROIT STORY"

IMAGES OF A LOST DREAM

ATTEMPT 2

MY MOTHER IS DEAD

"Realizing as I grew up that my Mother is deceased and what that really means for my life has not been an easy pill to swallow"; as a matter of fact my granny used to have to break and crush my

Images of A Lost Dream Page 39

Aim High or Die
"A true Detroit story"

Tylenol, because I couldn't or wouldn't swallow a pill. I know that's strange. I do not believe I will ever quite get over the fact that through life's hard, happy, sad, or just regular times I will not ever in this lifetime be able to have my mom. I ride past where she is buried on Detroit's East Side on Mt Elliot and Edsel Ford Freeway and I say, "Hello mother," that is about as good as it gets. Sometimes I wish I were right there with her. This is the second attempt to finish what I started. Today I went to school to register for classes and I was running off at the mouth as always; the man who sat next to me was a fellow student whom Mr. Black, my advisor, had introduced to me on a prior occasion. "Hey!" I said, you're here to get registered too I assume, and went on to say this is what the cover of my book will look like, watch for it; and this is me and the man that killed my mother. He said, "What is this guy's name" and at the same time we said "Gregory Aineesom." What a small world. He went on to talk about his friend Gregory Aineesom and his personality. In his own words no consolation to you, but he loved your mom, and was a nice guy. If he had only known, that I assumed so, but wondered what had changed all that. Okay, sorry to take you all over the place, but that happens to be a personality trait; we have yet to see if that is a flaw or an attribute. I did to not finish my semester due to financial problems and of course getting depressed, as I always do when Christmas, Thanksgiving, and the Holiday season rolls around, as it will do every year. I need to get a grip on this. I pray to God that I will make it, and not perish like most artistic and genius minds who battle with focusing on one thing at a time, and get something done instead of going over the same thing over and over again and not seeing any results. Hey, that happens to be the definition of insanity. I need to

Aim High or Die
"A true Detroit story"

practice what I preach. The good news is that I landed a little waitress job at a local diner and I met a man name Good News Will, a big guy in weight and in height at first impression. I was waiting on my section, walked past his table, that wasn't in my section, and he grabbed my wrist and began to say, "God is telling me to deliver this message to you, this year 2007, seven meaning completion." "This is your year of completion." "Whatever it is that you want, give it all to God, and watch your cup run over". He had chills on his arms and it sent chills down mine. We both began to cry; I suddenly remembered that I was at work. I thanked him and asked him to please stop because I didn't want to get fired from my new job. He responded, "You won't be here in a week anyway"; "whatever it is that you're doing it will sell millions of copies". The fellow, better known as "Good News Will," delivered his news. I was shocked that he knew, without my telling him, anything about my being and artist and trying to write a book. Sure enough, I wasn't working there in a week. I began that January to put all my focus on Aim High the artist. I had just spent all the money I had saved to rent a place, but I had to move out because of a slum landlord. My uncle was upset with me for supposedly breaking him up with his girlfriend because I came home from work every day and gave her money to drive her van. My own van, which I purchased from a nice man at work for five hundred dollars, had a gas leak that I hadn't had fixed yet. To be honest they needed the money because they were struggling too. Then my uncle put eggs in my gas tank, and sliced my tires because she told him that she wasn't allowing him to drive her van anymore, until he got a job. To top this all off with whipped cream and cherries; my granny didn't believe me when I told her what he did,

Aim High or Die
"A true Detroit story"

because he said that he didn't. I had to junk my van, move into my granny's house, where I was not comfortable, and ended up in the streets; literally sleeping from pillow to post and staying out in the studio, or sleeping on the couch or on the floor of friends, who did what they could, but needed their space as well. Other obligations were set aside to help me. I found my voice but I was at the lowest point ever. Things could only get better and they did. I stared recording songs; then I took it to the next level and began to perform at every open MIC club I could find.

I started soliciting DJ'S in Detroit to play my songs, and it worked. I formed partnerships with local promoters and began using advertising in flyers and banners and some television spots as well. I performed at least twice a week for the entire year as well as on Halloween, Christmas, and New Year's Eve. I was on cloud nine, a local celebrity, almost a local household name. Once I was out with a friend, and we went to a house party. A female in the party shouted, "That's you, that's the girl I was telling you about", speaking to her boyfriend, "you was performing at Plan B; don't be mad when you see me stepping in singing my songs". Wow! Did that feel good but it was almost normal then to hear comments like that.

Aim High or Die
"A true Detroit story"

"AIM HIGH OR DIE"

"A TRUE DETROIT STORY"

IMAGES OF A LOST DREAM
ATTEMPT 3

September 11th

Aim High or Die
"A true Detroit story"

This is the third attempt to finish what I started three years ago.

I thought I had it bad; you never quite realize that it may be nothing compared to what's coming next. Why can't we all just appreciate what we have and not worry so much about what we don't have? Have we for one second realized that our past is a testimony of our future, and what makes us who we are? I love me now more than I have ever loved myself, but in a friend's words" love you enough." I'll get back to that a little later. I've realized over the attempts that my mother's sudden and tragic murder affected more than me; in all reality I wouldn't feel the full impact until the present day. My granny lost her only daughter, first born, and so did my Big Daddy. My Father lost his wife and mother of his daughter. My uncles lost their only big sister and idol. My mother had such an impact on everyone she came across, some in negative ways, but mostly positive ways. I can recall so vividly one of my aunties saying to me, "I didn't like your mother, she thought she was all that" and my response even as a kid, saying to myself, "maybe she was." I've been going through so much with my family, trying to get answers to questions that have been on my mind since my childhood nightmares, questions like, "Why was I treated different."" Why was I not supported in my school functions," Why did my step-grandfather, RIP, put me out when I was sixteen

Aim High or Die
"A true Detroit story"

and say to my granny, "Let her go, she ain't going to be shit, just like her mother. On that note, why would anyone in their right mind talk badly about a deceased woman to her child. What happened to the saying," If you don't have anything good to say, do not say anything at all. I truly in my heart feel, that some people in my life just had so much hate for my mother, that they took things out on me. My aunt cut my hair, dressed me down, and tried to size me up with her daughter. My cousins were jealous of me because I had pretty hair, and was light-skinned; they teased me and called me, "white girl." They lied to their parents about my participation in school functions when I needed them for verification. Kids in my school use to ask me why my family didn't buy me "Fresh" clothing, I was always in "hand me downs", but I made the best out of it. I didn't have underclothes, and would take a pair from my cousin. She had more than she needed; things with the tags still on, and she would come to school and embarrass me by yelling, "Why you got on my panties", or her outfit. I could not believe it. I would not have wished my situation on anyone, but I wish they could have walked in my steps or slept on my palette for one day.

"Well it's all good, because I kept on pushing, I knew that one day I was going to be able to share this story, and hopefully help people who may have hurt me unintentionally to see what words can do to someone. Sticks and stones may break your bones, but words can also hurt you."

Images of A Lost Dream

Aim High or Die
"A true Detroit story"

I would go on to finish high school with offers to run track in college, but I was tired I guess, of all the discipline. In retrospect, I think because of a lack of support from family, I just felt like a failure. I thought that I knew what was best for me, and running my way through college was something that I did not want to do. I was stuck on poetry, rapping, singing, and trying to get it now. In 2001 I was a freshman at Northwood University. On September 11, 2001 I was directed to the television in our common area to see the towers falling. This is how I felt, and what I immediately did was to go to my dorm room in complete silence. I wrote an entire piece without stopping for a break…

The Pen Brings The Pain

The pen brings the pain buried in my veins

Amazing ways crazy days still I raise and give praise

For it is the best thing possible

There is no need for the hospital

Cops get him, lock down for a while

Never forever it's not the end so don't frown

But get down on your knees

Aim High or Die
"A true Detroit story"

By any means necessary

There is no question there so
together today/ if there's a will there's a way

Lord I give thanks

But why/why did that child have to die

Never a question why

Everything's for a reason why you're wheezing

No joke so don't joke

Go elope lift your spirits high

Whichever way you please

So times you got to eat what you can't stand the way I feel about peas

Your life

But remember his way

Today it's like this give thank for blessings

Aim High or Die
"A true Detroit story"

Never wish reminisce hug and kiss

Make up not Mac never look back

Shots in at the buzzard in just enough time

In the same second a crime left a young blind

Innocent suffers from others uneducated mothers

My brothers and sisters the child suffers

Let's eliminate the war come together that's clever for our souls we adore

Or there be more things to come it will only get worse

It's written in history to be the world's curse

As I count the cars that follow the hearse

Witness the stars fall from the sky

Men and women running scared

And we all know why

Times up days no more as tears pour of praise amazed

And most of all ashamed for we've sinned

Aim High or Die
"A true Detroit story"

Rise & AIM HIGH

Aim High or Die
"A true Detroit story"

Aim High or Die

"A TRUE DETROIT STORY"

IMAGES OF A LOST DREAM

ATTEMPT 4

New Orleans

Aim High or Die
"A true Detroit story"

I felt like I had to get out of my city, the city I loved, the city I was born in.

Everything reminded me of a past bad memory. Everyone in my close circle reminded me of a hurtful moment or time in my life. People who were supposed to support me were against me, calling me crazy, bi-polar, and making fun of a situation that was nothing like funny. Yes, I had to cope with my fears, pains, and transgressions, by drinking, smoking, and thinking that I needed love from a man, to make my pain go away. I never realized until now how promiscuous and radical my behavior was. I sought help from Judge Twin who became an influence in my therapy, and even after thinking that I wanted her help; I abandoned her help. I do not know why I ran away from people who truly cared and wanted to make sure that my future was bright, wanted me to finish school and become the best that I can be. In retrospect I feel bad for it but I turned out to do well on my very own. I was in a restaurant and seen a sign for Essence Music Festival and I thought maybe this was my opportunity to do something positive for my career. It turned out to be positive for not only my career but for my growth into the woman I have become.

Aim High or Die
"A true Detroit story"

On Mon, Jun 23, 2008 at 1:53 PM, Aim High <aimhigh313@gmail.com> wrote:

---------- Forwarded message ----------
From: Nick Thomas <EMFVolunteers@rehage.com>
Date: Sun, Jun 22, 2008 at 9:31 PM
Subject: Essence Music Festival | Internship Program | Letter of Acceptance
To: EMFVolunteers@rehage.com

More information will be emailed to you in the next few days. Dear interns~

Congratulations! You have been accepted into the 2008 Essence Music Festival Internship Program. Based on your applications, I know that each of you will be a great addition to the Essence team. If you also applied to be a volunteer, please disregard any emails regarding the volunteer program.

The next step is to attend the mandatory meeting this Wednesday June 25th from 6:30pm to 8:00pm at the Louisiana Superdome.

If you know anyone else that would like to intern, please let them know that a limited number of internships are still available, and ask them to visit www.essence.com/essence/emf/volunteer.html and submit an application no later than midnight on Tuesday June 24th, 2008

Images of A Lost Dream

Aim High or Die
"A true Detroit story"

UPTOWN RECYCLING Back to School.....
Gives Back...............

Well you can't say no one cares; I went to the first annual Uptown recycling Back to school rally right in the Heart of the old Calliope projects held in a vacant lot for the good of the community. There were awards for kids for good grades and each of them received a much-needed boost for their upcoming School year. Hundreds of kids assisted by their parents enjoyed the giveaways, a recyclable bag with the much needed school supplies to have a productive year, paper, notebooks, folders, pens, and pencils. There were a multitude of things to do as well, like catching a Motivational Speaker Speech, listening to some positive soul, having some down home red beans and rice, or a snow cone. Children waited patiently in line to receive a beautiful face painting, or a sculpted balloon by the clowns or take a train ride through the lot and bounce around in the Spider Man Giant Bouncer. The excitement and appreciation was written all over the kids' faces, as rainbow smiles and silly faces grinned on the cheeks of little girls who are certainly innocent and more important, our future. Community leaders such as the Hispanic Community Representative, was one of many who took the time to make this event collective by doing their part in the community showing a small but strong presence. "Not talking about it, Being about it", at this Grand Positive event in the Black Community where, astonishingly, there

Aim High or Die
"A true Detroit story"

was no presence of local mainstream media. However significant that is the show must go on and so the Shack Brown Drill Team showed us some much- needed disciplined behavior at their Sargent's command and put on a step show for all of us. Issues such as the rising epidemics of HIV/Aids in the Black Community was also addressed with a Samaritan van present to give free and confidential Testing to sexually active teens, and to provide information on the prevention and treatment of this horrific problem facing the Black Community every second of the day. Well, in a normally dark and life-taking neighborhood, here was life, and light. The hours were, filled with hope. The future community leaders were actively involved with the children that they were destined to help. Our children really do appreciate when someone cares; not when it may be too late and they are facing jail time or dead. This day did not go unnoticed by the many who were in attendance. The cars passed by, and the children went home that night exhausted from all the running around, excitement, and the love that the day brought. I give this event a remarkable two thumbs up, and would like to say thank you on behalf of the children. It is true that a little love extended to them will go a long way, letting them see that someone out there in the midst of all the chaos confusion and hate actually still loves.

Aim High or Die
"A true Detroit story"
Republican Party trying to suppress the Michigan Voters

Right now the Nation is at a moment of panic as bailout after bailout award CEOs of companies who practice an unsafe and Vegas style form of politics. In return, they gain from the worst economy we have seen since the great depression. Why then are there efforts underway right now in Michigan led by the Republican Party Chairman James Carabelli to suppress the important vote of many Michigan voters who have recently lost their homes due to the foreclosure crisis that has affected homeowners everywhere. In such a critical election every vote counts and these crucial voters are more than likely the voters who are tired of the George Bush's economic policies and are therefore some of the hardest hit by eight years of Republican led Washington. These tactics are not just criminal, in my opinion, but they are designed to keep change from happening when we need it the most. We all are aware that Michigan is a key battleground state that in the past has voted Democratic, and has a Democratic Governor. Major media outlets are showing that the McCain-Palin campaign is trying to turn this blue state red. "Lose your Home, Lose your vote", is the scheme that targets most Americans in Michigan and most Americans in a hard hit economy. I wonder then why this is happening in one of the most important battleground states. Something needs to be done, Michigan; we cannot sit back and allow Michigan to be stolen. With so much going on and devastation in many families' everyday living, do we expect voters, with less than forty-four days remaining in the election campaign, to pay for lawyers to investigate

Aim High or Die
"A true Detroit story"

their right to vote? This is sick Michigan, and we deserve better. This is the most important election in our nation's history and it is too important for any voter to be silenced. Does the Republican Party Chairman have a clue that Michigan is one of the hardest hit, most devastated, states hit by the Bush McCain economy and the home foreclosure crisis? This is un-American in a time when every vote counts for the Republican campaign to capitalize on a problem that they started and now want foreclosed homeowners to continue to suffer by taking away their right to change.

Obama-Biden has a plan that will benefit 95% of American families, but we need Michigan to see this through.

Someone do something!

By, Angel Marino

Americans have spoken; we now have our first black President in the White House. Excitement and rejoicing by the people who have chosen to make history. It has truly been a long journey to make it to this point. Slavery, The

Aim High or Die
"A true Detroit story"

Civil Rights movement, times in our nation's history that seem like just yesterday are now in the past; but let us not forget the road we've traveled as black Americans and as Americans alike.

I am writing this letter to address Americans but more significantly to speak to the millions of black Americans who suppose that the end is near. Hey listen, not the end of all things but the end of all our problems as black Americans in the political, economic, and social world. The reason I am concentrating on black Americans as opposed to other Americans is probably already understood; but to the majority of black Americans this might register to you and me as being a "sell out." Allow me to paraphrase a significant quote that Barack Obama has used on stump speeches and in his historic Democratic Nomination acceptance speech, "It is up to all of us Americans as well to do our part." Barack Obama was in the position to run for the highest position in the land, because he put in the effort to attain a college degree, go to Harvard law, run to become a state legislator and then become a United States Senator. Just like many of us, he was not raised with a silver spoon in his mouth; he was like many of us, raised mostly by a single mother, and then by his grandparents, and remembers how it felt to be the only black kid in school, or other places. Now he can be a blueprint and an example of what we can accomplish if we too put our minds to it and dedicate ourselves to something. Hard work and determination will lead you to the moment in life that you dreamed was yours.

So please, as politicians like to say, "Do not expect a golden parachute to bail you out of a crisis", we must look

Aim High or Die
"A true Detroit story"

at ourselves from inside and out and clean up our closets. We are killing ourselves, dependent on welfare; it does not seem like there is an end in sight. We blame all of our problems on the "white man." We do not take responsibility for our own lives. We have so many options now available to us with the Student loan Program, Grants, Scholarships, joining the Armed Services, Community Organizations are willing to help; yet we would rather steal from someone who has worked hard for the American dream, or blame someone for our faults. No, I am not saying that there aren't any hardworking educated black Americans who do not fit in this category, because there are millions of black Americans who have not only worked hard but who have strived so that the next generation will have it better than those before them. So if this pertains to you, I need you to know that we owe it to our forefathers, we owe it to the millions of successful black Americans who get stereotyped everyday as being like so many of us, young mothers, inmates, drop-outs, and all of the unfortunate people, who make up the mass of our race. We also owe it, more importantly, to ourselves. Someone said to me that some movie producers were looking to re-make the Jetsons and that they were only casting a few white people, and this guy says to the producer, "why is that there aren't any Blacks in the Future. Call it what you want, but we have the power to change, we have to stop living and dying by materials that we don't own drugs, guns, and Alcohol. Think about the past, now do you want a future?

Aim High or Die
"A true Detroit story"

TWO BLACK MEN..............
ONE WHITE
AMERICA..................................
....

Breaking News all around the Country finds black men in court rooms and on the run for crimes that range from Petty Larceny, Capitol Robbery, Rape, Murder, Drug Trafficking, and a multitude of other crimes to Misdemeanor and Felony. This Happens not to be a new phenomenon but rather it is something that has been going on in this country for over three-hundred years, reminiscent of the days of slavery when black men where stereotyped as animals, rapists of slave masters women, and fugitives for seeking freedom. What then happens to the black men, the few in corporate America, politics, and business, the many who try so hard to rid themselves of this genre and rather choose to try to live the American dream, life, liberty, and the pursuit of happiness? Many movies have been produced that depict black men as violent, misogynistic, rapists, drug dealers, and abusers, gives the perception to people of all races that there are no professional or working class black men. The role of

Aim High or Die
"A true Detroit story"

professional black men is slowly coming to the big and small screen with black men playing doctors, lawyers, and even presidents, but it is quickly over-shadowed by the BET countdown and the host of reality shows that reminds me of Black Face. Rarely, movies are produced that tell a slightly different story, the box office hit, "The Pursuit of Happiness", starring Will Smith, a highly successful recording artist, actor, and professional black man I might is one such. That movie being one of not many productions that showcase the real lives of many black men across the country, who desperately seek to gain honorable positions, and struggle to raise their children alone. This Story is about two black men from two different parts of the country who have two things that I know of in common; one being mayor of arguably the two most crime infested cities in America, and the other being black.

Mayor of Detroit Kwame Kilpatrick my Home city, and Mayor of New Orleans Ray Nagin my sister city, are two history making, highly motivated, educated, elected officials of two lovely historical cities, idols of many in Black America, and the prototype of what a black man can achieve in America. So then, tell me, why are the breaking news headlines, "Mayor Kwame Kilpatrick released from jail, ordered to wear a tether, and not to travel," after violating the terms of his bond by traveling to Canada for official city business, without the court's permission; after being charged with perjury, for testifying under oath that there was never a party in the Mayor's mansion, and why is Mayor Ray Nagin appearing in front of City Council to discuss NOAH funds, after being accused of mishandling funds. For as long as there has been law& order, government, and the press, we the people are entitled to democracy; we appoint our officials from the very top,

Aim High or Die
"A true Detroit story"

President, Commander in Chief, all the way down to our governors, mayors, and block club presidents. "The people have spoken," "innocent until proven guilty" must not apply to these two mayors. With Mayor of Detroit Kwame Kilpatrick's trial underway and Mayor of New Orleans Ray Nagin's controversial issues, I am apprehensive that there is no way, "innocent until proven guilty" will apply, rather "guilty until proven innocent "seems the rule. The tenacity of the media to have a good story, and have good ratings causes problems, because it leads the people to presume their guilt. Ignorance causes people to prefer to have a good soap opera right before their very eyes, "Misery loves company," rather than do their own research. We are now relying on the mainstream media and the internet for answers. Well it definitely makes great daytime and late night news. The problem is it is not at all what it seems people. In Spike Lee's words, "WAKE UP." In my own words, "GET YOUR MIND RIGHT". So it seems to me that your choices are limited, Black men, do not expect to find a job when you come out of prison. More important, stay in the ghetto in every urban area in every urban city and do not attempt to break the stereotypes. There is no a place for you in "White America."

To sum this up, what I'm trying to relay is this, in "Corporate America" in "Working Class America", and the "Streets of America," we've all heard the saying, "It's not what you know but who you know," "I'll scratch your back, you scratch mine". Hypothetically speaking let's just say, that if these accusations are proven to be true; what have both parties done that hasn't been done before? "There is nothing new under the sun," "let him who is without sin cast the first stone", and I bet you can't cast a

Aim High or Die
"A true Detroit story"

pebble. We've all done it before. "Hang them, why don't you". Everyday someone is hired in a company, not because they were the best candidate for the job, but because of a "Hook up", a connection, someone they knew. If we are going to prosecute these two men we need to take another look at ourselves as well as a better look at the top; it goes on in government, politics, religion, and in our everyday lives every day, from the top of the social ladder all the way down to the bottom.

[Here is one great example the war in Iraq, and George W. Bush.
I hate to be the one to assume but maybe there too powerful and too Black in White America.
Theoretically speaking.]

AIM HIGH OR DIE

"A TRUE DETROIT STORY"

IMAGES OF A LOST DREAM

ATTEMPT 5

Aim High or Die
"A true Detroit story"

Images of A Lost Dream

Page 63

Aim High or Die
"A true Detroit story"

Angel Marino why I Love you…...By, You

You like to stick to your own business and leave the power struggles to others; you know who you are, and what you believe in, but you do not see any reason to impose your values on everyone else. You generally don't get involved in organizing or motivating people, and you don't feel the need to always be seen as a big public decision-maker. You are also an honest, fair person. You don't lie or cheat to get ahead. You treat others with respect and hope for the same in return. You do not feel that you are above the rules that everyone else follows; you are definitely not willing to do whatever it takes to get ahead. You are a quick study. You generally don't need to have things explained to you more than once. When presented with a problem, you will often have an instant understanding of where to look for the solution. You do not take your sweet time when presented with a new task to complete or problem to solve. You don't avoid assignments that require you to learn new skills. You tend to hold onto your thoughts until you have something important to say, and even then you're not comfortable imposing your ideas on others unless you know they're truly interested. You don't enjoy talking for the sake of talking, and you have no desire to be the center of attention. Most important and why I love you, you have a genuine

Aim High or Die
"A true Detroit story"

interest in other people. You are a natural host, and are always thinking about how you can increase the happiness of those around you. When friends have problems or are in trouble, you're usually the first person they turn to for aid and comfort. You don't always say exactly what you're thinking; you don't like the idea of causing anyone pain because of your criticism.

Scoring high on the "warm" trait suggests that you are among those who enjoy domestic activities — doing things around the house —helping others, and making the world a better place. I love you.

Attaining the American Dream!

If I can make it here, I will make it anywhere,

New York, New York

The dream, more importantly your dreams, the ones you have been dreaming since you can remember having a dream. May I ask what you were dreaming, what were you

Aim High or Die
"A true Detroit story"

dreaming of? Well, for me I can honestly say I have always dreamed of being a successful powerful woman in my day; a genuine humanitarian, free of guilt or shame, full of integrity, pride, and strength, surrounded by loved ones. In my dream it is the result of hard work, faith, determination, charity, and will power to have this dream become reality. Dreams are sequels, you never know what's coming next, so you can hope for the best, aim high, and dream as big and as great as you like. So I am here in the big city, a student at Mercy College, a distinguished, private business school! What a way to dream you think! Optimistic and excited about my plans to graduate from Mercy College and begin my professional business career in New York. I want you to know, that first and foremost I am humbled and thankful just to be able to be a student and to still be optimistic about my future in spite of the knowledge of my past. I am grateful to be alive and every day that I remain in the race to attain the dream I am thankful. I am Angel Irene Marino from Detroit, Michigan where I was born and raised. My mother was Demeatrice, Exie, Marino, rest her soul. Life was tragically taken from her. When she was twenty years old, she became a victim of domestic violence and was murdered in front of her two-year-old child. I have defeated odds and barriers placed before me, and I am sincerely ready to make my collegiate career a defeated barrier. That's the way of attaining my dream. I am a journalist, I constantly sit back and take in life's never ending issues or questions to make sense of all of the mess, and drama, and hate, and of all things not good in the world. Hey, I'm not insinuating that everyone is perfect, but I am hoping that we can strive to be better. I am almost exalted on financial help to support me in funding my education; this is an independent attempt to give me a

Aim High or Die
"A true Detroit story"

chance. I am asking for a sequel in my dreams, the spin off to the nightmare I face if I cannot fund my education. When I was a young freshman, eighteen years old, attending Northwood University, a private school, I was not properly advised, unaware, and with little support, yet I stayed determined. I transferred on the advice of a guidance counselor who knew my situation financially, to a public school back in the city, Wayne State University. I want nothing more but to move on with my life, and be able to fund my education at Mercy College, to attain my BA in Media Studies/Radio TV. I wish to move on to become a Mercy Alumni and a successful powerful woman in my day, a Genuine humanitarian, free of guilt or shame, and full of integrity, pride and strength, surrounded by loved ones and sweet images. Now my dream is a reality, and it is the ultimate result of my promise to be a hardworking student determined to graduate, with the will power to see this dream become reality. I have nothing in Detroit, but memories of the mother that I lost and dreams of doing great things, so her death will not have been in vain. Please, please help me, because honestly, without a scholarship, I am not going to be able to pay for school.

GUILT………………..

What you waiting on, your thoughts are true

Aim High or Die
"A true Detroit story"

Your feeling real bad, well what did you do?

It's done………

No, you're thinking I could've but I didn't

Steady wishing now hoping and reminiscing

I should have done that, but I rather do this

Not one thought said sat

Now you sit ………….down

Meditate ask forgiveness for all

Don't look back stand humble but tall

Peace for all

Be a witness

You're not the only

It's the test in testimony

To help yourself

But to also help many

Please… May I

Aim High or Die
"A true Detroit story"

Eliminate Give me

Stop the fear

It's deadly

Cursing so many

There's enough to go around, it's provided, there is plenty

Empty, Nope the glass is full, but it's all in Perception, guilt is not your friend it's only
Deception……………………………………….

I CAN'T TELL………………..

I can't tell………..

America home of the brave, home of the insane
Institutionalized, stripped of our name

I can't tell……….

Land of the free, place of unity

Pride & dignity

Aim High or Die
"A true Detroit story"

I can't tell……………

Home of the free, liberty don't see

Prisons for you and me

Graveyards full of dead

We the People we said

Oh say can you see.

But I can' tell……………………….

Wars schools closed

Liquor stores build up (Bu)

Health diminish down

Bomb ties the sound

Pop pop from the guns

Aim High or Die
"A true Detroit story"

It's not fun

I can't tell…………………..

We want change but we remain the same

Point the blame

So much to say

Identity stolen still Holden on to it

Where did it go?

Who ARE YOU

ANGEL MARINO, NORMAN BENGE, ELEANOR LAIDLER

Do you even know……………………………………….

……..

Aim High or Die
"A true Detroit story"

"AIM HIGH OR DIE"

"A TRUE DETROIT STORY"

IMAGES OF A LOST DREAM
ATTEMPT 6

I am a Mother now

Aim High or Die
"A true Detroit story"

Arriving in New York City for the very first time was like being born again for me. The first thing I remember was the beautiful sky-line. I knew that New York was a magical place, what I didn't know is that the magic was going to be in the form of a child. Meeting Demi's Father Jai was one of the best things that could have happened to me In the Big Apple. Jai is a very wise, intelligent, man, indeed, he taught me things, introduced me to a new culture, and showed me how important it is to take care of your mind, body, and soul. The first six months we took on an extensive fast, no meat, no dairy, no soda, nor candy. What we put in our bodies was grown in the garden in the backyard. I was taught all the nutritional values of wheatgrass, and began growing and consuming it. Jai also taught me that if you have plans, put them in writing, Aim High daily on your plans. We would awake every morning at 5 o'clock AM and start our day with meditation. Television was not available, only loads of books to read, and every night and day I would get a book off the shelf and read, learning new information from genres all around the spectrum. It was not until we went out to a Trinidad party and had such a good time that I felt I was falling in love with Jai. It was one night of passionate love and Demi was conceived, of course it took 30 days before I was to see positive on the home pregnancy test. I was so scared yet very happy, I knew this had to be God, and God would make it all right. Jai fed me fresh fruit, vegetables, and warm soymilk that he made fresh daily with his soy joy machine. I felt like a queen and knew that I was carrying a princess who would one day succeed me. The great city of New York taught me many lessons, one being that hard work pays off. Everyone in New York seemed to be so driven to me, "Busy" taking care of business, minding their

Aim High or Die
"A true Detroit story"

own business, and rising early to start the day. The train would always be filled, and there were so many creative ways to make, what my friend Professor Charles Redmond calls, "Right now money".

This chapter is short because there is a completely new book about the whole story. The best thing to come from this entire trip is my daughter. I would return to Detroit with some real responsibilities. First things first, Demi's life must be better than mine. That is why this book ends with a finish project. I must finish things, complete my plans, and clean out my closet. This is detrimental to

Aim High or Die
"A true Detroit story"

securing a bright future for my Rose.

Images of A Lost Dream

Aim High or Die
"A true Detroit story"

Aim High or Die
"A true Detroit story"

"AIM HIGH OR DIE"

"A TRUE DETROIT STORY"

IMAGES OF A LOST DREAM

Attempt 7

Aim High or Die
"A true Detroit story"

Aim High or Die
"A true Detroit story"

Images of A Lost Dream

Aim High or Die
"A true Detroit story"

Images of A Lost Dream

Aim High or Die
"A true Detroit story"

Images of A Lost Dream

Aim High or Die
"A true Detroit story"

Aim High or Die
"A true Detroit story"

DEMI ELLA ROSE MARINO

Aim High or Die
"A true Detroit story"

Aim High or Die
"A true Detroit story"

Aim High or Die
"A true Detroit story"

Images of A Lost Dream   Page 86

Aim High or Die
"A true Detroit story"

Dear Love:

First, I must say thank you for braving that certain trip to Detroit in the midst of that woman's selfishness. Again, Every blessing for your enduring kindness.

Please let us accomplish the following before you return to our arms this weekend:

A. Close Proctor; (we need to know closing attorney)

B. Get the status of Ardmore - demand to speak to the bank holding "your" money; and

  Try to close before you leave for LA again on Friday;

C. Re-assign to more talented agent;

D. Get a new list so that we can select five more immediately;

E. Make calls to city regarding "Train Station." Who is the official in charge...?

Aim High or Die
"A true Detroit story"

F. Contact the Greenhouse people;

If you can see if your sister can help and we will give her a few dollars when she gets here.

I thank you and please stay healthy and safe! And when you get your $$$ from Ms. Walker please invest some into some Aim High promo for NYC subway ... stickers or similar tool and get you a $99.00 Pollstar AR directory. Now you can't say that the you cannot accomplish your Dreams. It's right before you. Love Jahi

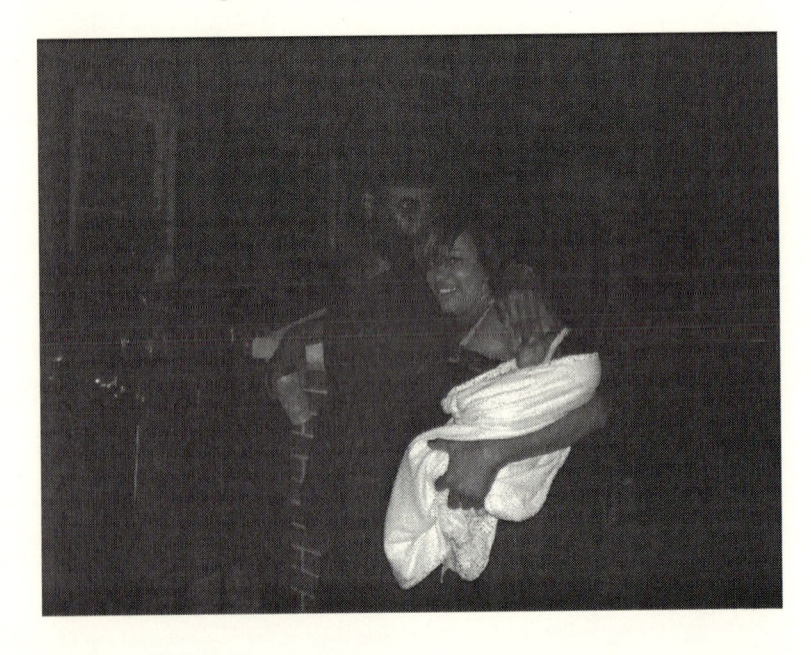